# HUATYA CURI AND THE FIVE CONDORS

*Tucoy hinantin huc yuric canchic.*
We are all one family.
                    *Paria Caca's Law*

*Huatya Curi and the Five Condors* is based on an unnamed myth from the *Tratado of Huarochirí* manuscript, written for Francisco de Avila in 1608. Manuscript included in *Narratives of the Rites and Laws of the Yncas*. Translated and edited by Clements R. Markham. London: Hakluyt Society, 1873.

This myth is from the Huarochirí of Peru.

© 1999 The Rourke Press, Inc.

ILLUSTRATIONS © Charles Reasoner

**Library of Congress Cataloging-in-Publication Data**

Lilly, Melinda.
    Huatya Curi and the five condors / retold by Melinda Lilly;   illustrated by Charles Reasoner.
        p.  cm.—(Latin American tales and myths)
    Summary: Huatya Curi, also known as Potato Eater, son of the mountain spirit Paria Caca, challenges a greedy king and wins a worthy bride, releasing his father from his icy mountain prison.
    ISBN 1-57103-263-0
    1. Quechua Indians—Peru—Huarochirí—Folklore. 2. Quechua mythology—Peru—Huarochirí. 3. Incas—Peru—Huarochirí—Folklore. [1. Incas—Folklore. 2. Indians of South America—Peru—Folklore. 3. Folklore—Peru.]  I. Reasoner, Charles, ill.  II. Title  III. Series: Lilly, Melinda. Latin American tales and myths.
F2230.2.K4L535  1999
398.2'08998323—dc21                                                    99–12101
                                                                                        CIP
                                                                                        AC

**Printed in the USA**

Latin American Tales and Myths

# HUATYA CURI AND THE FIVE CONDORS

## A Huarochirí Myth

Retold by
Melinda Lilly

Illustrated by
Charles Reasoner

The Rourke Press, Inc.
Vero Beach, Florida 32964

A long time ago, at the jagged top of the world where the snow lives, there was a poor young man named Huatya Curi. His name meant Potato Eater, for he lived off the vegetables that he found in the mountain fields of the Yauyo villagers. His name also meant orphan, because love for him was a cold wind, not a gentle touch.

He had no mother and his father Paria Caca was the spirit of the Andean highlands. Paria Caca could make a storm to shake the snow out of the sky. He could make a baby appear on a mountaintop and name him Huatya Curi. But he could not embrace the son he had made.

For as long as anyone could remember, Paria Caca had been held inside five enormous eggs balanced on the twin peaks of Condor Coto Mountain. The old stories said Paria Caca was imprisoned because his people were divided—scattered across the landscape without a word to say to one another. Mighty yet powerless, he waited for the people of the valley and the wilds of the highlands to become one family. Only then could he enter the world.

5

One day, after cleaning his hands in the fresh snow, Potato Eater ran his fingers over the giant eggs that held his father. A freezing wind swirled around him and he shivered as he recognized Paria Caca's breath.

"Father, Great Paria Caca, the Spirit of the Mountain," said Potato Eater, stretching his arms wide to embrace the wind. "Everywhere I look I see beauty, yet I am alone. Help me find the one who will share this beauty with me."

As if in answer, the wind grew stronger, whipping through Potato Eater's hair. His body shook with the gusts, but he held his ground. "Father, why—" he began to shout, but the wind snatched his words. Snow and ice battered him. At last he hurried down the slope, chased by icy blasts.

As he struggled to stay ahead of the chilly wind, he stumbled on a *guanaco* skin. It wrapped around him like a blanket and he fell, rolling and bouncing down the snowy mountainside. He came to a stop on a narrow ledge that overlooked the steep fields of the Yauyo Valley.

Potato Eater lay still, gasping for breath. He heard footsteps approaching and pulled the guanaco skin tightly around himself so he wouldn't be noticed. Peeking out, he saw a pair of foxes. One carried a panpipe flute and the other a *wankar* drum. He listened as they talked about a terrible sickness attacking the Yauyo Valley's new chief.

"It's no surprise Chief Kama Chiq is sick," said one of the foxes. "He'd no sooner been named chief than he took the people's lands and llamas for himself. Greed like that calls the monsters of disease. And now he's offered his beautiful sister Chaupi Ñaca as wife to anyone who can heal him."

The other fox sighed, saying, "She's lovely. Her hair gleams like a condor's feather and is so long it nearly sweeps the ground."

Unable to contain himself anymore, Potato Eater leaped out of the skin. "Tell me more about this woman, Chaupi Ñaca!" he cried.

"Yip! Yip! Yow!" squealed the pair. "It's not a guanaco, it's *runa*! A man! Potato Eater man! Hurry! Yip!" They raced away, dropping the panpipes and drum in their panic.

Potato Eater picked up the instruments. "Thank you, Father Wind," he said. "I'm glad you put me in the foxes' path. I see you've brought me the drum and flute for my journey." He played his new flute, imagining that the lilting melody sounded like Chaupi Ñaca's voice. As he headed down the highlands into the valley, his heart beat as fast as his drum.

Once in the village, he came upon a group of well-dressed Yauyo clansmen. "I am Potato Eater, son of Paria Caca," he announced. The people giggled at his strange name and ragged appearance. "I've come from the mountains to cure Chief Kama Chiq."

"The wise men of the Andes have failed, but you think you can succeed?" scoffed a richly adorned healer. "Well, no one's tried moldy potatoes yet." Trailed by laughter, Potato Eater continued on to the grand house of the chief.

As Potato Eater stepped up to the house, he was met by the most beautiful woman he'd ever seen or imagined. Her eyes shone like polished stones and her face seemed lit from within.

"Greetings, my name is Potato Eater," he said humbly. "I've come from Condor Coto Mountain to heal the chief." The beautiful woman, Chaupi Ñaca, didn't laugh, for she saw a strength and nobility in him that no one else had noticed. Smiling gently, she introduced herself and led him into the murky chamber where the sick chief lay half asleep.

Potato Eater waited for his eyes to adjust to the dim light. Starless nights on the mountaintops had trained him to see shapes in the darkness: the black wing of a condor, the Hunter's Stars, and the swirling shapes of the spirit world. He looked intently for pattern and movement. There! On the ceiling and the floor shadows twisted and breathed. Potato Eater looked closer. Over the chief's bed coiled two enormous snakes, ready to devour him. At his feet a two-headed toad waited with mouths open.

"Chief Kama Chiq," said Potato Eater. "Can't you see that your greed has called the hungry snakes and toad to your house? They take your spirit from you just as you took land and animals from the villagers."

Looking up, the chief fixed his eyes on Potato Eater. "Liar!" he exploded. "You sent these monsters to attack me, stranger!" His tirade ended in a burst of uncontrollable coughing. "Now get rid of them!"

"Are you still offering your sister, Chaupi Ñaca, in marriage to the one who heals you?" Potato Eater responded.

"Yes, of course, of course," coughed the chief, waving him away. "That's what I proclaimed, isn't it?"

"Then I'll hold you to your promise," Potato Eater said.

14

Whirling like a winter wind, Potato Eater grabbed the coiling snakes and the two-headed toad. The astonished villagers gave way as he charged outside and hurled the monsters out of the valley.

Chief Kama Chiq stepped from his house. "My people, I am healthy once again," he announced in a strong voice. Then he pointed his finger accusingly at Potato Eater. "This evil man," he declared, "sent monsters to make me sick. How easy it was for him then to cure me."

Kama Chiq glared at Potato Eater. "Marrying my sister won't be so easy," he warned. "You must prove yourself. Bring your drum and flute to the plaza tomorrow and we'll see whose music is more powerful, yours or mine!" He brushed Potato Eater aside, saying, "Now get out of my sight."

17

The next morning, Potato Eater joined the crowd already gathered in the plaza. Noting his arrival, Kama Chiq raised his hands and quieted the villagers. Then he lifted a panpipe flute to his lips and led the people in song. The women drummed, the men played their flutes, and the children danced. Music and color filled the valley. Finally the song faded into stillness and Kama Chiq pointed his flute at Potato Eater.

All eyes were on Potato Eater as he walked alone to the center of the plaza. He set down his drum and lifted his panpipes. He looked up at his mountain home, remembering snow swirling in the wind. He breathed in the chill, closed his eyes, and began to play. His music rose up, whipping through the sky like a blizzard.

The villagers gasped as the beautiful Chaupi Ñaca joined Potato Eater, picking up the drum at his side. She pounded it with the strength of a condor's wings. The villagers, the dirt, the stones, the clouds, and finally Earth danced to the song of Chaupi Ñaca and Potato Eater!

"AIIEEE!" screamed Kama Chiq. "*Pachaq kuyukuynin*! Earth moves! Stop! Stop! You win!"

Once the shaking had ended, Kama Chiq declared, "Thanks to my sister, you've passed this test, Potato Eater. But anyone who would marry her must have the dignity and look of a chief." He smoothed his fine tunic. "Tomorrow we celebrate the corn harvest. If you don't have anything to wear but rags, don't bother coming."

That night Potato Eater climbed up to Condor Coto. "Great Paria Caca," he called. "I need clothes befitting a chief." An icy wind circled around him, covering his torn rags like a snowy blanket.

The next day, Kama Chiq came to the plaza in all his finery. He strutted past the piles of ripened corn while the villagers admired his tunic of feathers and gold. Brimming with pride, he looked across his new fields and noticed a blinding white light coming down the mountainside. "A shooting star!" he cried. "Headed for us!"

The crowd hushed, awed by the sight. Shielding his eyes from the brilliance, Kama Chiq squinted and saw the light wasn't a star at all. It was Potato Eater, dressed in a tunic of ice that dazzled in the sunshine.

20

"You've dressed well today," admitted Kama Chiq as Potato Eater entered the plaza. "But I have a final test. A Yauyo should provide a home for his family. Let's see who can build the finest home in the shortest amount of time."

"I've passed all your tests," said Potato Eater. "Kama Chiq, you promised that once I healed you I could marry your sister, Chaupi Ñaca. A chief should keep his word. After I win this last contest Chaupi Ñaca and I will wed."

Kama Chiq seethed as he listened to the villagers murmur their agreement. "My people," he barked, silencing them. "Gather the smoothest rocks and straw. Find the finest stone masons and the most skilled weavers. We have a house to build!" The villagers scattered to fulfill his orders.

All day long Potato Eater calmly watched the construction of Kama Chiq's house. At sunset, he examined the nearly completed building that shone in the sunset like gold. "Chief, are these walls strong enough to keep out the wind?" he asked.

"Sun himself could live in my home and never fear the winter storms!" Kama Chiq boasted. "Workers, return at dawn to put on the roof. We're finished for the day," he proclaimed. "And you, Potato Eater, are simply finished. Not one stone has been laid for your hut!" Smiling with self-satisfaction, he led his workers back to the village plaza.

23

While stars glimmered in the clear evening sky, Potato Eater returned to the highlands. Lifting his panpipes, he called all the creatures on the slopes of Condor Coto to help him with his house. Guanacos and *vicuñas* brought piles of stones on their backs. Foxes and snakes smoothly fit the rocks together to make walls. Birds fluttered above, weaving the roof. Potato Eater and the animals worked all night.

When Sun rose over the mountains the next morning, the villagers stepped out of their homes and blinked in surprise. Potato Eater's new house was as beautiful as Condor Coto itself. The walls were as smooth as its icy cliffs and the roof of woven feathers glowed like the rainbow that stretched between the twin summits.

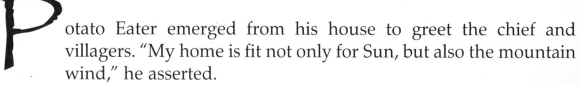

Potato Eater emerged from his house to greet the chief and villagers. "My home is fit not only for Sun, but also the mountain wind," he asserted.

"You've finished first," Kama Chiq conceded, glancing over at his incomplete house. "But your walls are thinner than the skin of an old potato. Of course the wind will live here. This shanty will fall down with the first storm."

"We'll see," Potato Eater replied. He lifted his flute, again thinking of the whipping winds that howled between Condor Coto's peaks. The breath from his flute grew until it became an icy gale pounding against his house, but the walls stood strong.

The wind twisted in the air and then battered Kama Chiq's unfinished home. Straw flew off the partly woven roof. Rocks groaned against each other. In a clatter, they tumbled off the walls, making muddy piles.

The wind spiraled over the wreckage and turned to blast Chief Kama Chiq. He dug in his heels, but the gale pushed him across the plaza, out of the village and up the mountain trails to Condor Coto and beyond. He was pushed so far away that he never returned.

otato Eater slowly lowered his flute and took Chaupi Ñaca's hand. Together they walked to the twin pinnacles of Condor Coto. At the mountaintop they stood together as one while the wind embraced them in a circle of powdery snow. Potato Eater and Chaupi Ñaca were married.

"Father," said Potato Eater, "love has made the people of the valley and the wilds of the highlands into a family. We are all one and you are free at last." His words echoed between the peaks of Condor Coto and cracked the five eggs.

Five grown condors flew out of the broken shells and carried the new couple back to the village below. When they alighted in the plaza, the people welcomed them with cheers. "All honors to our new chief, Potato Eater! To his wife, Chaupi Ñaca! To the great spirit, Paria Caca!"

"At last they see you as I do," said Chaupi Ñaca and smiled.

The five condors rose above the village. Their wings covered the sky with blessings as they soared over the upturned faces of Potato Eater, Chaupi Ñaca, the Yauyo villagers, and the mountains and valleys—one land at last.

30

# PRONUNCIATION AND DEFINITION GUIDE

**Chaupi Ñaca** (chah OO pee NYAH kah) — a legendary Yauyo woman

**Condor Coto** (KON dor KOH toh) — a Peruvian mountain

**guanaco** (gwah NAH koh) — a wild llama of the South American highlands

**Huarochirí** (hwow roh chee REE) — an ancient highland culture of the Andes, the Huarochirí became part of the Incan Empire.

**Huatya Curi** (HWAH tcha GOO ree) — a legendary Andean mountain man associated with the Huarochirí people

**Incas** (ING kahs) — people of the Andean highlands, the Incas established an extensive empire that flourished before the Spanish conquest. Their language is Quechua.

**Kama Chiq** (KAH mah CHEEG) — Quechua for chief

**pachaq kuyukuynin** (PAH chag koo yoo KOO y neen) — Quechua for earthquake

**Paria Caca** (par EE ah KAH kah) — the main god of the Huarochirí, Paria Caca was also worshiped by the Incas and Yauyos.

**Quechua** (ge CHOO ah) — the language of the Incas, Quechua was adopted by all in its empire, including the Huarochirí.

**runa** (ROO nah) — Quechua for man

**vicuña** (vee KOON yah) — a wild relative of the llama

**wankar** (WAHN kar) — an Andean drum

**Yauyo** (YAW yoh) — a culture and people of the Peruvian valleys